MEET THE STARS OF PROFESSIONAL

WRESTLING

Motrin

MEET THE STARS OF PROFESSIONAL

WRESTLING

By James Patrick

SCHOLASTIC INC.
New York   Toronto   London   Auckland   Sydney
Mexico City   New Delhi   Hong Kong

The wrestlers described in this book
are trained professionals. Don't attempt
to imitate the dangerous feats they
perform in the ring. Please, stay safe, and
leave the stunts to the professionals.
—JP

COVER PHOTOS
The Dent

No part of this work may be reproduced, or stored in a retrieval system, or transmitted in any form or by any means, electronic, mechanical, photocopying, recording, or otherwise, without written permission of the publisher. For information regarding permission, write to Scholastic Inc., Attention: Permissions Department, 555 Broadway, New York, NY 10012.

ISBN 0-439-21629-X

12 11 10 9 8 7 6 5 4 3 2   0 1 2 3 4 5 6/0

Printed in the U.S.A.
First Scholastic printing, October 2000
Book Design: Michael Malone

The BOTTOM LINE

Professional wrestling is riding a **wave** of **popularity. A wave?** Later for that. Let's call it what it is — a tsunami crashing **down** on **contemporary pop** culture with the force of ten thousand **piledrivers.** Wrestling is every-where you look nowadays — on **weekly television** programs, **pay-per-view** specials, comic books, action **figures,** best-selling **biographies, advertisements, video** games, CD-ROMs, websites, even feature-length films.

The one **wrestler leading the way?** That would be a guy named Dwayne Johnson. But he's not the only one riding the **wave.** There's a **bevy** of **behemoths backing him up:**

Stone Cold Steve Austin,™

Mankind,™

Goldberg,™

Triple H,™

Bret "The Hitman" Hart,™

The Undertaker,™

and more. Excuse me? What's that? Dwayne who? Oh, you probably know him as...The Rock.™

PHOTO: Duomo/Steven H. Sutton

Just how popular is The Rock?

Well, how much time have you got, jabroni? Forget the number one *New York Times* best-selling book. Forget all the fans (the millions...and millions) repeating his catchphrases. Forget the movie offers, gargantuan book signings, and endorsement deals. Forget, even, the stint hosting *Saturday Night Live*. All you've really got to know is that he recently appeared on *The Martha Stewart Show*— that's right, Martha Stewart, America's last line of defense against poor taste and lousy flower arrangements. The Rock and Martha, it's the zaniest pairing since pizza and broccoli. But wait,

there's more. Turn on *Nash Bridges* and you'll see Stone Cold Steve Austin in a recurring role (he plays a rule-breaking cop who's got a problem with authority – go figure). What's next, America? The Undertaker on *The Rosie O'Donnell Show*?

There's just no stopping the wave. It keeps building power and momentum. Wrestling is everywhere. It's mainstream entertainment. And guess what? It's only going to get bigger.

The action in the ring is dramatic, sensational, more exciting (and dangerous) than ever. The wrestlers are clearly superior athletes and talented showmen. Meanwhile, the stunts keep getting wilder.

But it's not just the wrestling that's gotten wild. It's the ever-changing storylines, the soap opera, the characters. Fans love to follow the twisting, turning, complicated plots, the feuds between wrestlers, the battles between brothers, the surprising comic performances — *the show business of it all.* And make no mistake: Professional wrestling is a "sports entertainment," not an athletic competition. The feuds are mostly crafted by creative staff writers. The results of the matches are planned in advance. Nope, it's not about who wins and loses. It's about entertaining the audience, by whatever means necessary.

The fans have spoken. Leonardo DiCaprio and *Titanic* are history (besides, who'd he ever beat, anyway?). Professional wrestling is the real BLOCK-BUSTER of the day. So sit back, relax, grab a bag of popcorn, and enjoy the show.

PHOTO: The Dent

WRESTLING LINGO

THE LOCK-UP: At the beginning of a match, when two wrestlers join in a clench.

BABY FACE: A good guy. But wrestling today is changing. Sometimes the fans don't like the baby faces. Fair and honest, they can seem a little dull.

HEEL: A bad guy. In wrestling today, we often see baby faces turn into heels, and heels suddenly become baby faces. It's part of the soap opera.

RUNNING SPOTS: A spot is any specific wrestling move. "Running Spots" is any sequence of moves that take place in the ring.

PUT SOMEONE OVER: To let an opponent win a match, according to plan.

LAY DOWN THE BELT: To put someone over in a title match. It's simply seen as part of the business.

SELLING: To help make the action seem more real, more convincing, the wrestler — like a movie actor — will pretend he's in terrible pain. That's selling.

He drips
with
ego,
CONFIDENCE,
and **PURE ATTITUDE—**

and he can back up
every word...
if you **smell** what
The Rock
is cooking.

The ROCK

Height: 6'5"
Weight: 275
Born: 5/2/72
Hometown: Miami, FL
Birth name: Dwayne Johnson
Website: www.therock.com

PHOTO: Duomo/Steven H. Sutton

This book is not sponsored or endorsed by the WWF, WCW or ECW.

From elbow to eyebrow, The Rock's got it going on.

He's the "People's Champion," the self-proclaimed "most electrifying man in sports entertainment." Not that anyone is going to argue with him. After all, they don't call him The Rock for nothing. The man is built like a boulder. A former football star at the University of Miami, where he played defensive tackle and wore #94, The Rock's dream of playing in the NFL was derailed by injury. The Rock felt sorry for himself for about a minute and a half. Then he set a new goal; he decided to follow his father's footsteps and become a professional wrestler. In 1996, at age 24, he became the youngest man to win the Intercontinental Championship. In 1999, as the World Wrestling Federation (WWF) World Champion, he headlined the main event at *WrestleMania XV* against Stone Cold Steve Austin, in one of the most memorable matches in *WrestleMania* history. Impressive, you bet. But it's his skills with the mike that may be The Rock's greatest talent. He's the undisputed King of Catchphrases. And these days The Rock can't start a sentence without 15,000 fans finishing it for him...

"If you can smellllll... WHAT THE ROCK IS COOKING!"

Signature Move

Take your pick, The Rock's got a couple. There's "The Rock Bottom" and "The People's Elbow." Both can leave an opponent stunned, making for an easy pin.

PHOTO: The Dent

"KNOW YOUR ROLE AND SHUT YOUR MOUTH."

THE ROCK IS THE ONLY THIRD-GENERATION WRESTLER IN THE WORLD WRESTLING FEDERATION. BOTH HIS FATHER ROCKY JOHNSON, AND HIS GRANDFATHER HIGH CHIEF PETER MAIVIA, WERE TITLE HOLDERS.

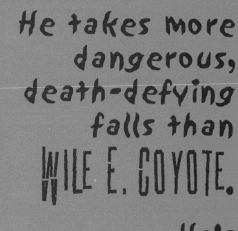

He takes more dangerous, death-defying falls than WILE E. COYOTE.

He's **Mankind** and he's made a friend with pain. Better look out, though. Because here comes...

Mr. Socko™!

This book is not sponsored or endorsed by the WWF, WCW or ECW.

MANKIND

This book is not sponsored or endorsed by the WWF, WCW or ECW.

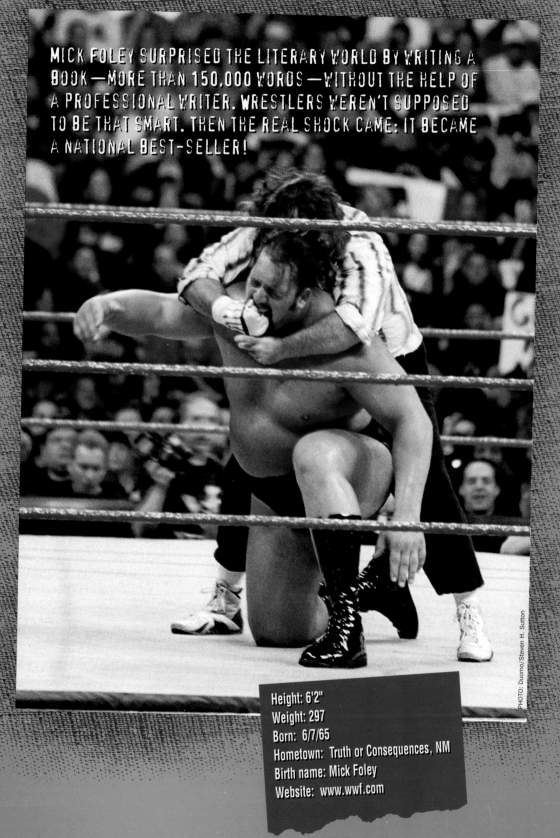

MICK FOLEY SURPRISED THE LITERARY WORLD BY WRITING A BOOK—MORE THAN 150,000 WORDS—WITHOUT THE HELP OF A PROFESSIONAL WRITER. WRESTLERS WEREN'T SUPPOSED TO BE THAT SMART. THEN THE REAL SHOCK CAME: IT BECAME A NATIONAL BEST-SELLER!

PHOTO: Duomo/Steven H. Sutton

Height: 6'2"
Weight: 297
Born: 6/7/65
Hometown: Truth or Consequences, NM
Birth name: Mick Foley
Website: www.wwf.com

PHOTO: The Dent

Mick Foley has wrestled under the names Cactus Jack, Dude Love, and—most notably—Mankind.

Sometimes all in the same month! By all reports he's an intelligent guy, a loving husband and father. He likes ice cream, amusement parks, and watching cartoons. That's one side of Mick Foley. The other side—the wrestling side—is another story altogether. He's known as the "Hardcore Legend." A guy who thinks nothing of taking a twenty foot dive off a steel cage into a table, or down on a mat covered with thumbtacks. He lost two-thirds of his right ear in a 1994 match in Germany. He's suffered through more injuries than most football teams endure in a season. What's more he's something of a creative genius. With Foley's latest invention, the so-called "Demented One," Mankind wears a loopy, lopsided smile and a leather mask. Two years in a row (1998 against The Undertaker, and 1999 against The Rock) Mankind participated in ring wars that were named "Match of the Year" by *Pro Wrestling Illustrated* magazine. No matter where, no matter when, Mick Foley (under any name) always goes all out. It's made him popular with a lot of doctors around the world—and a lot more fans, who know they can always count on Mick to put on an incredible show.

"HAVE A NICE DAY."

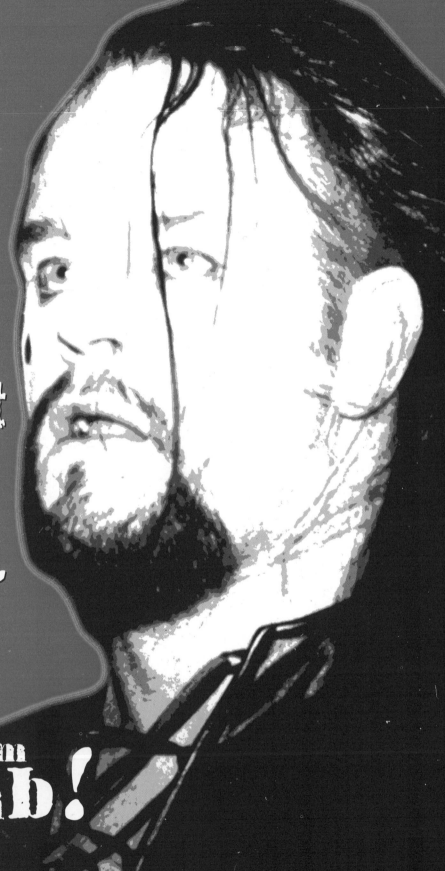

After years in the ring, his body's beaten up. He's had surgery on his hip and knees.

But he's not buried yet.

And even if he was, The 'Taker is one dude who would definitely rise from the tomb!

The UNDERTAKER

PHOTO: The Dent

MARK CALLAWAY, WHO WRESTLES AS THE UNDERTAKER, PLAYED COLLEGE BASKETBALL AT TEXAS WESLEYAN UNIVERSITY IN FORT WORTH. HIS POSITION? C'MON, DO YOU HAVE TO ASK? CENTER, OF COURSE!

Height: 6'10"
Weight: 325 pounds
Born: 3/24/62
Hometown: Death Valley, AZ
Birth name: Mark Callaway
Website: www.wwf.com

When Mark Callaway, wrestling as The Undertaker, first joined the WWF in 1990, most people didn't know what to think. Because here was something frightening and new. Sure, the WWF had always featured outrageous, colorful, outsized personalities. But The Undertaker was a step beyond; he was a "character." An invention. There didn't seem to be a real person underneath, as compared to, say, Jesse "The Body" Ventura or Jake "The Snake" Roberts. Callaway remembered those early days in an interview with *Wrestling Digest* magazine:

"I remember kids crying when they first saw me."

Smart kids, no doubt. He soon became a top draw, playing haunting heel against Hulk Hogan in some classic matches in '92 and '93. Over the years, his character has evolved, changing with the times. His feud with his manager Paul Bearer (get the pun, folks) and "brother" Kane (as played by Glen Jacobs), briefly turned The Dead Man into a sympathetic baby face with the fans. In early 2000, The Undertaker took time off from the wear and tear of the ring to nurse a series of back injuries. Plans are for him to return in a big way, because The Dead Man is one guy you can't keep down.

"THE DEAD MAN"

Signature Move

The Undertaker has this, well, little problem. He likes to bury guys. When he needs that finishing touch, The 'Taker often resorts to "The Tombstone Piledriver," giving the appearance of driving his opponent's head into the mat in one of the most fearsome stunts in professional wrestling.

PHOTO: The Tent

He's a throwback. **A tough guy** who **detests** flash and gimmicks. **GOLDBERG** just wants to lace 'em up and **get it on.**

He doesn't talk much, either. Just one question: **"who's next?"**

GoldBerg

PHOTO: The Dentt

PHOTO: The Dent

Height: 6' 4"
Weight: 285
Born: 12/27/66
Hometown: Tulsa, OK
Birth name: Bill Goldberg
Website: www.annihilBor@aol.com

Signature Move

When moving in for the finish, Goldberg features "The Jackhammer." An old wrestling move that had fallen out of favor, it's a combination vertical suplex and power slam. Goldberg updated it and brought it back— with a vengeance.

In an age when microphone skills often matter more than ring skills, when flashy costumes seem more important than genuine toughness, Bill Goldberg stands out like a throwback to the glory days of Bruno Sammartino and Pedro Morales. Just watch the way he snarls and charges the ring from backstage. No smiles, no showboating, no face paint. He's all business— 285 heavily muscled pounds of focus and bubbling rage. Despite the television cameras and screaming fans, Bill Goldberg goes about his job like a regular, working class guy—the only thing missing is the lunch pail and a hard hat.

A man of few words, he lets his matches do the talking. And they speak volumes.

After joining World Championship Wrestling (WCW) in September of 1997, he tore through the opposition like a tattooed tornado, winning 173 matches in a row before finally falling to Kevin Nash. A former NFL football player for the Atlanta Falcons, Goldberg was forced into retirement when an abdominal tear put him out of action. That's when he got his new job, wasting opponents in the WCW.

OUTSIDE OF THE RING, BILL GOLDBERG IS A BIG PUSSYCAT. HE WAS NAMED NATIONAL SPOKESMAN FOR THE HUMANE SOCIETY AND HAS TESTIFIED BEFORE CONGRESS IN HIS FIGHT FOR ANIMAL RIGHTS. HIS THREE CATS ARE NAMED MOE, LARRY, AND CURLY.

"WHO'S NEXT?"

They used to call him **Giant.**

Now he's known as **the Big Show.**

But for years, he was nothing but a big disappointment.

Then he won the **WWF CHAMPIONSHIP** belt.

The BiG Show

"LARGE AND IN CHARGE."

ON NOVEMBER 14, 1999, THE BIG SHOW BECAME ONLY THE SIXTH MAN TO HOLD BOTH THE WCW AND WWF WORLD CHAMPIONSHIP TITLES, JOINING BRET HART, HULK HOGAN, RIC FLAIR, KEVIN NASH, AND RANDY SAVAGE.

Height: 7'2"
Weight: 500
Born: 2/8/72
Hometown: Tampa, FL
Birth name: Paul Wight
Website: www.wwf.com

PHOTO: Duomo/Steven H. Sutton

Signature Move

Let's be honest: When you're 7'2," 500 pounds, do you really, really need a fancy move? Won't a boot to the face do just fine? But when push comes to shove, and shove comes to slam, The Big Show calls on "The Showstopper."

PHOTO: The Dent

It's hard to imagine a man of Paul Wight's stature not getting respect (at 500 pounds, he makes Shaquille O'Neal look like a schoolboy), but a fact's a fact. In the WCW, wrestling as The Giant, he never seemed to command the spotlight. So Wight bolted the WCW to join Vince McMahon's WWF. Wrestling as The Big Show, he made his first appearance at 1999's famous St. Valentine's Day Massacre, interfering in McMahon's cage match against Stone Cold Steve Austin. Still, there seemed something almost gentle about the giant. That is, until the Big Bossman started messing with his head. That seemed to awaken the big man from his slumber. The wrath he unleashed on the hapless, helpless Bossman made heads turn and tongues wag. In November of '99, The Big Show won a wild three-way match involving The Rock and Triple H, coming away with the title belt —and a whole new level of respect from fans and opponents alike. Though often playing a heel, The Big Show remains strangely innocent; no one's ever sure which way The Big Show will go. That's what makes him so dangerous. Lately, he's played sidekick to hard-nosed manipulator Triple H, but cracks appear in their unholy alliance. One thing's for sure, however: **The Big Show will be in the spotlight for years to come.**

At the dawn of the millennium, this hard-nosed **heel** was voted the **most HaTed man** in WWF wrestling.

THEN HE REALLY GOT MEAN.

TRIPLE H

33

HE USED TO WRESTLE AS TERRA RYZING IN THE WCW BEFORE MOVING TO THE WWF IN 1995. THEN HE WRESTLED AS HUNTER HEARST HELMSLEY. NOW HE'S TRIPLE H. IT SURE BEATS HIS BIRTH NAME— JEAN PAUL LEVESQUE.

Height: 6' 4"
Weight: 274
Born: 7/27
Hometown: Greenwich, CT
Birth name: Jean Paul Levesque
Website: www.wwf.com

After years of disappointment, great things finally seem to lie ahead for Triple H in 2001 and beyond. The WWF's leading heel (and dreaded leader of D-Generation X), Triple H put a major crimp in WWF owner Vince McMahon's life when he whisked off Vince's daughter, Stephanie, to a quickie wedding in a Las Vegas drive-in chapel. But Triple H isn't just soap opera and promos, he's participated in some of the fiercest, most exciting ring brawls in recent WWF history. In '99, he fought an outrageous No Holds Barred match against Mr. McMahon (including a garbage can, road sign, shopping cart, and car!), winning with the assistance of McMahon's own double-dealing daughter, Stephanie. This victory earned Triple H a title match against The Big Show. In January of 2000, Triple H won that match, and the belt, thanks in part to interference from Road Dogg, Billy Gunn, and X-Pac. Lately, his old feud with The Rock appears to be heating up again, big time.

Many wrestling observers feel they'll be battling for WWF domination for years to come.

"I AM THE GAME."

Signature Move
Triple H calls it "The Pedigree," but it's really a highly modified, extremely devastating version of the classic piledriver. Once Triple H locks it on, a chill of anticipation goes over the crowd. Then, BOOM, it's time for the fat lady to sing.

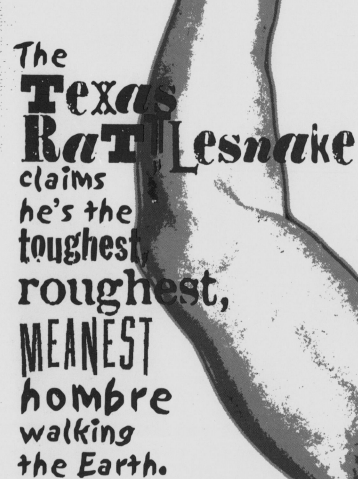

The **Texas RaTTLesnake** claims he's the toughest, roughest, MEANEST hombre walking the Earth.

And that's the bottom line, 'cause STone CoLd says so.

STONE COLD
STEVE AUSTIN

"'CAUSE STONE COLD SAYS SO."

PHOTO: Cuomo/Steven H. Sutton

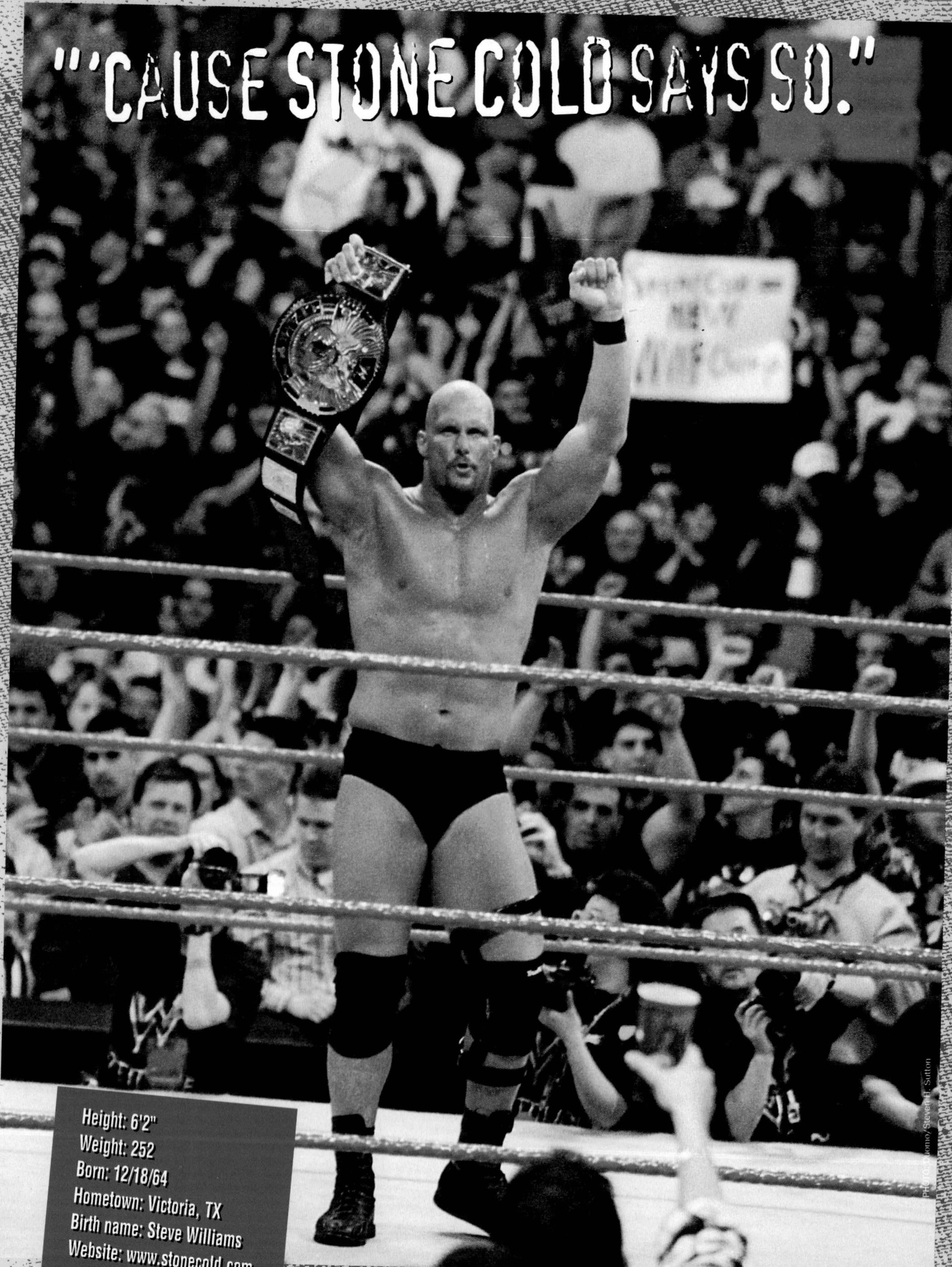

Height: 6'2"
Weight: 252
Born: 12/18/64
Hometown: Victoria, TX
Birth name: Steve Williams
Website: www.stonecold.com

Signature Move

Easily the most famous finishing move in the WWF today, "The Stone Cold Stunner" electrifies any crowd with its sudden, staggering force. After he grabs an opponent by the neck, Stone Cold snaps him face-first into the canvas. Night-night, lights out, sleep tight.

For Steve Austin, the road to superstardom has been long and torturous. He first turned pro in December of 1989. In the grinding world of a wrestler, that's thousands of nights in strange hotels, hundreds of thousands of miles to travel. It's impossible to calculate the countless piledrivers, forearm shivers, and bodyslams endured. Through it all, Steve's performed with class and professionalism.

A four-time WWF World Champion, he almost single-handedly brought wrestling to its current peak of popularity. Fans embraced his Stone Cold character. The ultimate rebel, a man who showed no respect for authority, no regard for the rules. Stone Cold trusted nobody—and he wiped the floor with any man who climbed through the ropes. But the road exacts its toll. After an Owen Hart piledriver went awry, Steve began to complain of pains in his neck. Finally, on January 17, 2000, Steve underwent surgery to remove bone spurs from his neck. His concerned doctors advised him to hang up the black boots forever. But that's not about to happen until Stone Cold says so. And chances are, he'll be back in the ring, coiled like a snake and fighting to reclaim his spot atop the WWF.

NOT ALWAYS THE BALD, ANGRY, TOUGH-TALKING, BLUE-COLLAR HERO HE IS TODAY, "STUNNING" STEVE ONCE WON A 1993 WCW TAG-TEAM TITLE WITH HIS PARTNER BRIAN PILLMAN, WRESTLING AS "THE HOLLYWOOD BLONDES."

His father, Stu Hart, trained wrestlers such as **Rowdy Roddy Piper, Davey Boy Smith,** and CHRIS JERICHO.

But **six-time World Champion** Bret Hart is perhaps the finest **pure wrestler** Stu's ever produced.

"THE HIT MAN" HART

"I'M THE BEST THERE IS, THE BEST THERE WAS, AND THE BEST THERE EVER WILL BE."

Height: 6' 1"
Weight: 234
Born: 7/2/57
Hometown: Calgary, Alberta
Birth name: Bret Hart
Website: www.wcw.com

PHOTO: The Dent

Signature Move

"His Excellence of Execution," as Hart is sometimes called, features more moves than a plate of Jell-O. He can beat you any number of ways. But his torturous submission hold, "The Sharpshooter," is undoubtedly his most famous.

Son of legendary wrestler Stu Hart, "The Hitman" is possibly the most skilled technician ever to enter the squared circle. Not the biggest or the strongest guy in tights, Bret is an "old school" wrestler who features an arsenal of maneuvers and can execute them all with peerless precision. Few can touch his ring accomplishments. Hart has won the WWF World Championship five times—first by defeating "Nature Boy" Ric Flair, back in '92, then beating Yokozuna, Diesel, and The Undertaker (twice!). In 1997, while feuding with Vince McMahon, Hart turned his back on the WWF and moved to the rival WCW. It wasn't an easy transition. Finally, late in December, 1999, Hart came home with a victory over Goldberg, and his first WCW World Title. So what could be left for this wrestling icon to accomplish? Well, "The Hitman" is a traditional kind of guy. Bret hates wrestling's current emphasis on gimmicks and soap opera. For Bret, pure wrestling is all that matters. For all the fans who still care about that kind of thing, just catch a match with Bret.

He wins the old-fashioned way: He earns it with blood, sweat, and guts.

BRET LOST HIS BROTHER OWEN HART IN THE WORST TRAGEDY EVER TO BEFALL THE WWF. WHILE MAKING A DRAMATIC ENTRANCE BY BEING LOWERED FROM A CABLE, OWEN FELL NINETY FEET AND CRASHED TO THE TURNBUCKLE BELOW. HE DIED INSTANTLY. SOMEHOW, DESPITE THAT, BRET'S MANAGED TO CONTINUE HIS CAREER IN THE RING.

Acrobatic aerials, backflips, and jaw-dropping leaps off the top rope?!

That's why JERICHO'S star is on the rise!

CHRIS JERICHO

PHOTO: The Dent

CHRIS HONED HIS ACROBATIC RING SKILLS WHEN WRESTLING IN MEXICO AS "CORAZÓN DE LEÓN." FOR THOSE OF YOU SCORING AT HOME, THAT'S HEART OF THE LION.

Height: 5' 10"
Weight: 225
Born: 5/9/70
Hometown: Vancouver, British Columbia
Birth name: Chris Irvine
Website: www.chrisjericho.com

He calls his fans "Jericholics." Actually, Chris calls everyone a Jericholic, since he naturally assumes that everyone is a fan. Brash and supremely confident, Chris showers himself with love on a daily basis. But he's much more than another egomaniac with a mouth and a microphone.

Chris Jericho has built a solid reputation as a strong, fast, agile, and fearless wrestler.

Though underweight, "Lionheart" will tangle with anyone, anywhere, anytime. An extremely technical wrestler, Chris turned pro before the age of twenty. And he's paid his dues, learning his craft by criss-crossing the globe, wrestling in Germany, Mexico, and Japan. That's where Chris adopted his high-risk, high-flying style. He's wrestled (and held titles) in the Extreme Championship Wrestling (ECW), WCW, and now the WWF—eventually beating Chyna to claim the Intercontinental Title in December 1999. Born on Long Island, Chris grew up in Canada, where he learned to love ice hockey. And why not? His dad is former National Hockey League star Ted Irvine, who played for the New York Rangers, Los Angeles Kings, and St. Louis Blues from 1967–77. Besides, they have some pretty decent brawls in hockey, too.

"THE AYATOLLAH OF ROCK AND ROLLAH."

Signature Move
He won the WWF Intercontinental belt by applying "The Walls of Jericho" to Chyna. But the "Lionsault" may be his strongest move, when Chris backflips off the second rope, crashing down on his forlorn foe.

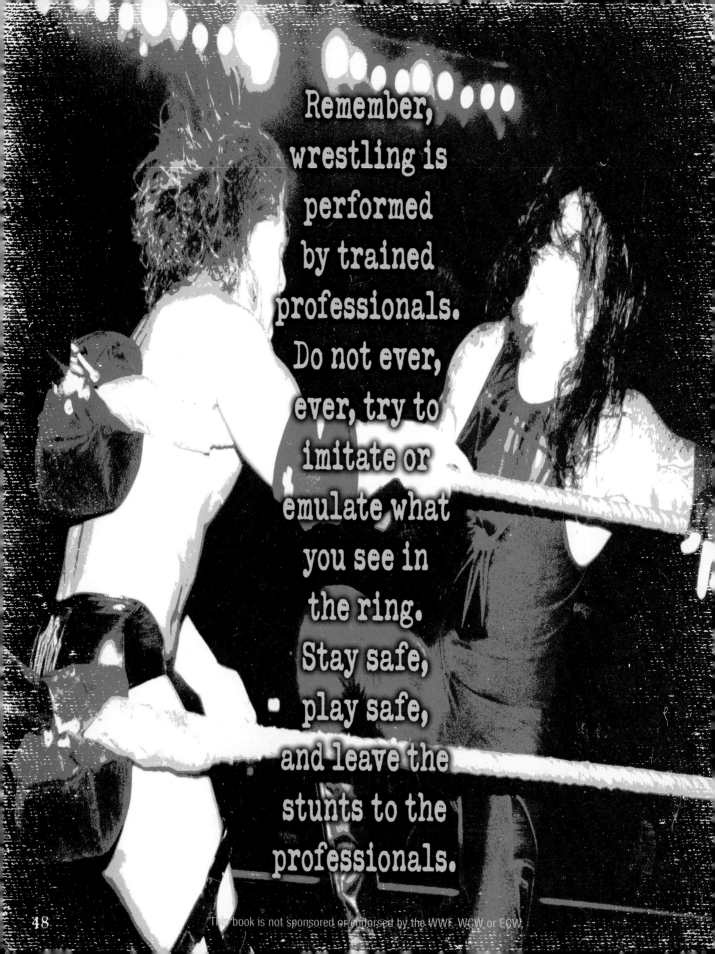

Remember, wrestling is performed by trained professionals. Do not ever, ever, try to imitate or emulate what you see in the ring. Stay safe, play safe, and leave the stunts to the professionals.